Contents

The origins of the war

On 28 June 1914 in the Bosnian capital, Sarajevo, a teenager called Gavrilo Princip shot dead the heir to the Austro-Hungarian throne, Archduke Franz Ferdinand, and his wife Sophie. This act marked a turning-point in world history for it sparked off a whole series of events that led to war. The First World War (1914-18) claimed the lives of nearly 10 million soldiers. The horror and misery of those caught up in this terrible conflict are almost unimaginable, but one way to gain a sense of what they had to endure is to read the poetry written during the war.

Some of the writers featured in this book were poets before they went to fight, for example Isaac Rosenberg and Edward Thomas (see page 15). Others turned to poetry during the fighting as a much-needed means of expression. Some, such as the women poets in this book, were not involved directly in the fighting yet still had to deal with hardships at home. Several of the poets discussed were also journalists, artists and musicians. Many were killed during the conflict.

> *We are the Dead. Short days ago*
> *We lived, felt dawn, saw sunset glow,*
> *Loved and were loved, and now we lie*
> *In Flanders fields.*
>
> From 'In Flanders Fields' by John McCrae

Archduke Franz Ferdinand and his wife Sophie in the Bosnian capital, Sarajevo, shortly before their assassination on 28 June 1914. The Archduke had decided to visit Sarajevo even though he had been warned of the dangers of the situation in Bosnia-Herzegovina (see page 7).

The balance of power

Why did Princip step out of the crowd of demonstrators around the Archduke's carriage with a gun in his hand on that fateful day in 1914? To understand what happened then and afterwards, it is necessary to look back at events towards the end of the 1800s.

Throughout much of the 19th century, countries in Europe maintained a balance of power that helped to prevent wars involving more than two or three countries. However, one war that did break out was a conflict between France and Prussia (a German state). This war ended in 1871 with victory for the Prussians, and the creation of a unified Germany. Many of the other European countries grew increasingly uneasy and fearful about this powerful newcomer, with its industrial might and well-trained armies. Countries in